# The Story of the U.S. Naval Academy

A NAVAL INSTITUTE BOOK FOR YOUNG READERS

# The Story of the U.S. Naval Academy

### Clara Ann Simmons

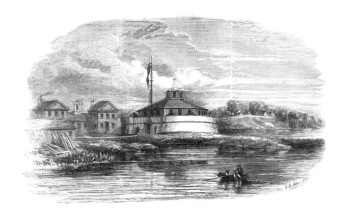

Naval Institute Press
*Annapolis, Maryland*

*Library of Congress Cataloging-in-Publication Data*
Simmons, Clara Ann, 1923–
    The story of the U.S. Naval Academy / Clara Ann Simmons.
            p.       cm.
    Includes bibliographical references (p.   ) and index.
    Summary: Presents an illustrated history of the 150 years of the United States Naval Academy at Annapolis, Md., by focusing on the lives of its midshipmen.
    ISBN 1-55750-767-8 (alk. paper)
    1. United States Naval Academy–History–Juvenile literature.
[1. United States Naval Academy–History.]  I. Title.  II. Title: Story of the US Naval Academy.
V415.L1S54  1995
359'.0071'173–dc20

                                                              94-48747

Printed in the United States of America on acid-free paper ∞

02 01 00 99 98 97 96 95       9 8 7 6 5 4 3 2
First printing

*To the Memory of*
*Lambert Wickes*
*and the young men of sail*

To: Greg
study hard at school!

Not your Dad,
Jeff Heiser

In preparing this book I have been the lucky recipient of the collaboration of Elizabeth M. Simmons. Her expertise as a youth services librarian, her knowledge of research resources, and above all, her unfailing joie de vivre have kept me afloat.

# Contents

# The Story of the U.S. Naval Academy

# To Be a Sailor

This is the story of the United States Naval Academy. The Academy is where young men and women are trained to become first-rate officers in the U.S. Navy. It all started a long time ago, in 1845, on Windmill Point in Annapolis, Maryland. By that time the United States was sixty-nine years old. It had had a navy since the Revolutionary War. Heaven knows the Academy should have been started sooner. The country always had needed good navy men. It had never sent them to school to learn to be sailors.

There was an old saying, "The best place for a young man is at sea." Hardly anybody thought sailors could be trained in school. The U.S. Congress had voted for an army school at West Point, New York, many years earlier. They said it would be undemocratic to have a navy school. One congressman exclaimed, "No, Sir!" They thought men sitting in college could not learn how to sail a ship in a storm.

The old sailors who had helped win the American Revolution knew the only way to learn to hoist an anchor, reef the fore topsail, or climb the mizzenmast was by doing it. They all had learned this way. Many of them began sailing when they were young boys.

The only way to learn to sail was by doing it. Young sailors reef the topsail and swab the deck.

Sometimes they left school when they were only ten years old and shipped out as cabin boys.

They lived on wooden boats not even one hundred feet long. Everyone was jammed in together with hammocks side by side. They froze in winter and steamed in summer. They ate salt pork, beans, and dry biscuits. They were flogged with a knotted rope if they did not work well. If they became good sailors, they were made first mates. After a while they were able to captain a merchant ship. They sold cargo all over the world and became rich.

One man who became captain of a ship was John Paul Jones. One of the Navy's greatest heroes, he is buried in the Naval Academy's chapel. You can see his green marble sarcophagus when you go to visit the chapel's crypt.

John Paul Jones was born in Scotland. When he was thirteen, he came to Virginia, where his brother lived. Later, when the American colonies went to war with Britain, he joined the new Continental Navy. On June 14, 1777, America's first flag day, he was made captain of the sloop *Ranger* and sent to France to fight in enemy waters. He had many successful raids against the British Navy.

Then he was given the ship *Bonhomme Richard* to captain. It was an old merchant ship made into a war ship and was named for Benjamin Franklin. Dr. Franklin was in France trying to get aid for the American colonies. "Bonhomme Richard" was the pen name he used when writing his *Poor Richard's Almanack*.

Jones sailed from France with a squadron of six ships into the North Sea off England's coast. There he met up with the British man-of-war *HMS Serapis*. The two ships began fighting each other. It was a fierce fight with the ships side by side firing cannon, muskets, and grenades at each other. The *Bonhomme Richard* was hit again and again. The captain of the *Serapis* asked Jones if he wanted to surrender. "I haven't begun to fight," he shouted back. He kept on pounding the enemy until their masts were broken, the ship was full of holes, and they surrendered.

On the deck of the *Bonhomme Richard* John Paul Jones yells to the captain
of the *Serapis,* "I haven't begun to fight."

John Paul Jones salutes the *Bonhomme Richard* as it sinks after it
defeated the British ship *Serapis.*

The only way to learn names like mainmast, mizzenmast, yardarm, and all the names of sails was by going to sea, the old sailors said.

Jones said afterwards that he didn't know as much about naval tactics as did other countries' sea captains. He believed that officers should be trained in mathematics and mechanics. He thought that each ship in a fleet should have a little school on board.

Not many people paid attention to this idea. They remembered the old saying about being at sea. But over the years more and more people began to think the Navy needed a training school. Alexander Hamilton thought such a school should be built. John Adams, who was president of the United States from 1797 to 1801, thought so, too.

President Adams decided to have a schoolmaster on each navy ship. America was a young country and didn't have much money. To save money, the ships' chaplains were told to teach writing, arithmetic, and navigation. Of course, they didn't know much about what they were teaching. As it turned out, they hardly got a chance to teach. Officers could call seamen from classes at any time to attend to ship duties.

More people kept trying to get the school. President James Monroe said it would be better not to have ships than to have them full of untrained officers. His Secretary of the Navy, Samuel L. Southard, asked the Congress four times to fund a naval school. Four times the Congress voted no.

Finally schools were begun on two old wooden frigates, the *Guerriere*, based in New York City harbor, and the *Java*, based at Norfolk, Virginia. Another was begun at the old sailors' home, the Philadelphia Naval Asylum in Philadelphia, Pennsylvania. School masters were hired to give midshipmen cram courses to pass the exam to become officers. Midshipmen didn't have to attend the classes. Often they didn't. It was more fun to go on leave and frolic on shore and in town. They trusted to luck at exam time.

In 1842 the Navy built a training ship. She was racy, built low to the water, and named the *Somers*. Her captain was Commander Alexander S. Mackenzie. She was filled to overflowing with teenage

Captain Mackenzie hanged the young upstarts. Two of them
look very small hanging from the yardarm, on the training ship *Somers*.

boys sent to learn seamanship. On her first voyage, some of these brash young boys tried to mutiny. They thought they could take over the *Somers*, become pirates, and get rich.

Captain Mackenzie was furious at this act. He had the upstarts put in chains and hanged the three ring-leaders from the yardarm. One of them was Philip Spencer, son of the Secretary of War. Mackenzie executed Philip Spencer and the other two sailors without a regular court-martial. A court-martial is a trial required by the Navy. When the newspapers reported on the hangings, the American people were furious. Again people said they needed a training academy on land.

They were about to get it because the days of sailing were coming to a close. Two years earlier the Navy had ordered its first three seagoing steam-driven vessels. They were powered by boilers that used coal or wood. They had new types of guns. Men couldn't learn to run them by furling sails, splicing rigging, and tacking to windward. Now seamen needed a school to learn science and engineering. People were excited about this new age of steam and said they wanted a school.

In 1845 President James K. Polk appointed George Bancroft Secretary of the Navy. He told his new secretary to improve the Navy in every way. George Bancroft was just the person to get an academy built. He had believed in education all of his life.

*Top,* Secretary of the Navy George Bancroft looked at Fort Severn on Windmill Point and decided that was the place for a naval school. *Bottom,* the Naval School in 1846. The mess hall is on the left and the classroom on the right.

# George Bancroft Gets a School

George Bancroft liked school. His father, who was a minister, taught him to read when he was very young. By the time he was six years old he was reading books that belonged to his father. In 1813, when George was only thirteen years old, he went to Harvard University in Cambridge, Massachusetts.

He was a very good student at Harvard. After he graduated, he was sent to Germany to study at Gottingen University. It was well known as a place for good students. He studied Latin, Greek, and ancient history, and decided to be a teacher. When he got back to the United States, he taught Greek at Harvard. His students made fun of him because he often said, "thus we do in Germany" and sometimes fell asleep in class.

In 1823 he decided to open his own school where students would have to work harder than they did at Harvard. The new school was called Round Hill and was for boys nine to twelve years old. In those days girls did not go to school as often as boys did. The students were taught to be on their honor to do their very best. Today the Naval Academy's midshipmen are taught the same thing.

At Round Hill the students had a strict daily schedule. They started every day at 6:00 a.m. with prayers. They didn't get breakfast until 8:00. All they got for breakfast was bread and butter, a baked apple, milk, and coffee. They wore uniforms and were not allowed to have pocket money. Today at the Naval Academy the midshipmen wear uniforms, can only have a little bit of pocket money, and start their day early.

By the time he became Secretary of the Navy, George Bancroft knew a lot about schools. When President Polk told him to make the Navy better in every way, he knew he wanted to start a school for sailors.

William Chauvenet was an excellent teacher and head of the school at the Philadelphia Naval Asylum. He wrote to Secretary Bancroft saying that a two-year school with regular classes should be started at the asylum. He did not want the students coming and going as they pleased. The other teachers at the asylum were Professor Henry H. Lockwood, Lieutenant James H. Ward, and Passed Midshipman Samuel L. Marcy, whose father was Secretary of War William L. Marcy. They were all good teachers.

George Bancroft wanted the school and he wanted those teachers. He didn't like the idea of having a school at Philadelphia. He looked around and came upon the Army's Fort Severn at Annapolis, Maryland. The Army had built the fort in 1808 to keep enemy ships out of the Chesapeake Bay. They weren't using it now. It was the perfect spot for a naval school. It was on Windmill Point on the Severn River, which flowed to the bay. It was a place where training ships could be docked. It had buildings that could be used for classes and to house the midshipmen.

Annapolis was an old quiet town that had been a port for two hundred years. The citizens were proud of their town. It was the state capital. Annapolis had been the capital of the United States for one year before Washington, D.C., was built. George Washington resigned as commander in chief of the Continental Army in

Annapolis's State House. Many important Americans built grand houses in the town. William Paca, one of the signers of the Declaration of Independence, built his big brick house on Prince George Street. You can visit his house and the State House when you go to Annapolis.

The people of Annapolis were used to seeing sailors in their port. George Bancroft thought it was the perfect spot for more sailors. But he wasn't going to ask the Congress for the money. No, Sir! They always voted "no." The Naval Board of Examiners was meeting in June 1845 to test the midshipmen at the Philadelphia Naval Asylum. Secretary Bancroft asked them to help him and they all voted "yes."

It was easy to get the Army to agree to give Fort Severn to the Navy. He just asked himself. It so happened that the Secretary of War, William L. Marcy, was on summer vacation. While he was away, Secretary Bancroft was to take care of his work. So Bancroft just signed his own name as Acting Secretary of War and transferred Fort Severn to the Navy.

There was $30,000 in the Navy's budget for education. Bancroft used this to get the school going. He assigned the four good teachers from Philadelphia to Fort Severn. He put the teachers from the other training schools on waiting orders. That meant he did not have to pay them, so he had enough money to get started.

In three quick steps George Bancroft did what men dreamed of for years. He opened the United States Naval School in Annapolis, Maryland, on October 10, 1845. The Navy honored him many years later by naming its largest building "Bancroft Hall." It is where the midshipmen live and eat and is so large that thousands of students live there. Part of it is built over the site of Fort Severn, which was torn down. You can see Bancroft Hall when you visit the Naval Academy.

Secretary Bancroft named Commander Franklin Buchanan as the first superintendent of the school. Buchanan had been in the Navy for thirty years. He was known as "an old sea dog" who did not think very much of young men carousing on the town. He was delighted to find that the new school was surrounded on two sides by water and on the other two by a high brick wall. That would keep the students in and they couldn't skip class and go to town for fun. The Academy is still surrounded by walls and water.

The midshipmen lived in barracks called "Apollo Row." The building was full of leaks. The students said they didn't mind getting wet when it rained. They did mind the snow blowing in because the building was so cold the snow never melted! There were buildings where the teachers lived, a hall for classes, and a house for the chaplain. At the very tip of Windmill Point was the round stone fort that was fourteen feet high and had ten guns.

Fifty-six boys entered the first class. They spent one year at the school, and went to sea for two and a half years. Then they went to school for another year to study gunnery, mathematics, and seamanship. If they passed the test at the end of the year, they were made lieutenants in the Navy. Sometimes the Navy didn't have room for more lieutenants. Then the students who passed were called "passed midshipmen." They were made lieutenants as soon as there was room for more.

Most of the fifty-six students came from the Philadelphia school. They had been used to a free and easy life there. They wanted to have fun at the new school, too, so they started Midshipman Simpson's Spirits Club. It wasn't long before they decided to give a party. On January 15, 1846, when the Naval School was just a few months old, they held a Grand Ball. They decorated the building with streamers and potted palms and served refreshments. People came from Baltimore, Washington, and Annapolis to enjoy the festivities and see the new school. The dance was such a big success that they kept having one every year.

On January 15, 1846, the midshipmen had a Grand Ball.

Superintendent Buchanan was delighted to find the school
surrounded by water and high walls. Building No. 4 is
Apollo Row, which leaked when it rained.

# Rowdy Times and Changes

Superintendent Buchanan worked hard to get the school started on a firm course. He made sure that the boys studied hard, obeyed orders, and attended to duty. After he had been there for about two years, he was called away by duty. In 1846 the United States went to war with Mexico to try to get Texas as a new state. Buchanan, the "old sea dog," asked to join his fellow officers at sea to fight the war. He was reassigned by the Navy and sent to sea. Ever since then, naval officers have served as superintendents of the Academy for only a few years at a time. Then they are reassigned by the Navy to some other duty.

Commander George P. Upshur was appointed in Buchanan's place. Upshur had been in the Navy for thirty-one years and was well liked. Alas, he did not know what it meant to be stern and firm. In no time at all the young midshipmen found that they could get away with all sorts of tricks. Midshipmen with good grades were given liberty to go into Annapolis. They were supposed to sign a liberty book before they went so teachers would know where they were. Just for fun, they started skipping to town without signing.

This was just the beginning. They started drinking clubs with names like Crickets and Owls. Every Saturday night they met in

Midshipmen skipped to town without signing out. Fifty years later they were still doing it by climbing over the wall.

someone's room. They sang songs and told tall tales. They drank whiskey and smoked cigars. They made all sorts of noise until after midnight. They left their rooms in a mess. Commander Upshur said he didn't know what to do! The boys would have to make their own rules.

Midshipmen on liberty in Annapolis fought with young towns-people. They fought each other in duels, which were against naval rules. In earlier times young, hot-tempered Navy officers had fought duels. Stephen Decatur, the famous hero of the raid on the *Philadelphia* at Tripoli during the Barbary Wars, was killed in a duel in 1820. He was shot on the dueling field at Bladensburg, Maryland, which is near Washington, D.C.

One of the Naval Academy's roads is named for Stephen Decatur. The Tripoli Monument is on the road. It is in memory of the six brave young officers who died during the Tripoli War. It is a Navy tradition to name a building, a ship, or a monument after heroes. You can see the Tripoli Monument on Decatur Road when you go to visit the Naval Academy.

Two midshipmen, Francis G. Dallas and John Gale, fought a duel on June 7, 1848, on the same field in Bladensburg where Decatur fought. Dallas was hit in the right shoulder. This fight finally was too much for Superintendent Upshur. He had both men dismissed from the school. That ended dueling. It didn't end the midshipmen disobeying orders.

In 1848 Professor Lockwood was told to teach military drilling for half an hour each day. He had graduated from West Point and knew about marching and gunnery. The school's Academic Board felt that drilling was good exercise. The midshipmen didn't feel this way at all. They called it "pig driving" and made fun of Lockwood by calling him "The Shore Warrior."

They also made fun of him in another way. Professor Lockwood stuttered. One day he started his battalion marching toward the Severn River. When they got near the shore, he started to order "Halt."

*Top*, Commodore Stephen Decatur, hero of the Battle of Tripoli. The
Tripoli Monument is on Decatur Road.
*Bottom*, The dueling field at Bladensburg, Maryland, where Stephen
Decatur was shot. Midshipmen Francis G. Dallas and
John Gale fought a duel on this same field.

All that he could stammer was "Ha-haw-haw." The midshipmen just kept right on going. They marched straight into the river, dragging the small cannons behind them. Of course they knew what they were doing. The next time Professor Lockwood stuttered over the word "Halt," they halted because they didn't want to get all wet again. Poor Professor Lockwood, for years midshipmen played jokes on him.

By late 1849 the Academic Board felt it was time for some changes. The school's name was changed to the United States Naval Academy and that is what it is called today. Students went to the Academy for four years and had three years of sea training. Today they go for four years and have sea duty after they graduate. They were given grades, with 4.0 being the highest grade they could earn. 4.0 is the same as an "A" and is the highest grade today. The board wanted just what Secretary Bancroft and Superintendent Buchanan had wanted, a firm course and a set of rules to be obeyed.

The Academic Board also decided that the midshipmen's sea training would be during the summer. They used a sloop named the *Preble* and in 1853 she sailed to the northern coast of Spain. The sloop was named for Captain Edward Preble, who had sailed to Spain during the Barbary Wars to meet his squadron. Stephen Decatur was one of the young officers in his squadron. So again, the Navy used the name of a hero. They also named a building for Preble. You can see Preble Hall on Maryland Avenue when you visit the Academy.

The Academy began to grow. Two plots of land that added thirty-three acres to the grounds were bought. A wooden wall and roof were built on the fort, which turned it into a big hall for gymnastics. There is a picture of a fencing class inside the fort. Swords must have been flying every way as there were over seven sets of men fencing side by side. Fencing was the first sport introduced into the Academy and is still a sport today.

Five new buildings where the midshipmen lived were built along the river. They were called Stribling Row and had ninety-eight rooms. Each room was for two students and had two beds and two

Stribling Row. Maybe these are the midshipmen who were studying
when they heard a loud crash and the back wall fell out.

A midshipman posing for his picture at the new Naval Academy in 1853.

chests of drawers. The students shared the other things in the room—a looking glass, a wash basin, a slop bucket, and a broom.

The students also shared something of the feeling of those who had lived in leaky Apollo Row. One evening when they were studying, they heard a loud crash. The whole back wall of one building had fallen out. The midshipmen found they were studying in the open air looking at the Severn! You can imagine how they hooted and hollered at this.

A large chapel with columns was built beside the old seamanship building. A recitation hall made of granite was built on the other side. The Academy was getting more and more modern. Steam heat and gas lights were put in the buildings. A small observatory was built. Land was filled in along the shore line so that a sea wall could be built.

After only fifteen years the Naval Academy looked like a first-rate military school. It had a campus of about forty-five acres, which is called "the Yard." There were over twenty new buildings. Most important, there were new courses and more teachers.

Then came rumbles of a new war, the War Between the States. It began in 1861 and changed the Academy for many years.

*Top,* swords flying every way at an early fencing class inside Fort Severn. *Bottom,* Fort Severn after it was roofed over and turned into a gymnasium.

The midshipmen studied gunnery and seamanship on the training ship
*Constitution*, which was moored at the Naval School.

# A Terrible Time

The War Between the States was a terrible time for the United States. The southern states wanted to break away and make a new country. The northern states didn't want this to happen. During the war men from the South fought men from the North. Often good friends fought against each other. It was a terrible time for the Naval Academy, too. Some midshipmen left to join the South in the Confederate Navy. Many stayed to fight with the U.S. Navy. Often classmate fought classmate.

Some of the officers and teachers joined different sides. Professor Lockwood left to join a Delaware state infantry regiment. He was the drill master whom the midshipmen made fun of when he stuttered. Perhaps he didn't stutter when he trained the Delaware soldiers. Commander Buchanan, the Academy's first superintendent, resigned from the Navy to join the South. He was from Maryland and thought his state would leave the Union. But Maryland did not leave the Union, so the school stayed in the care of the U.S. government. Although they were Marylanders, most of the citizens of Annapolis wished their state would join the South. They even threw rocks over the school's wall, because it was a school for the Union Navy!

This worried Captain George S. Blake, the superintendent of the

Academy in 1860. He was afraid they would try to attack the school and had howitzer guns placed at the gates. He was very worried that there would be a raid on the ship *Constitution*. This famous old wooden ship had been built in Boston in 1787. She was a beautiful, lean, and long frigate with three main masts. She was Edward Preble's ship when he fought the Barbary Pirates. She had been in forty-two battles, captured twenty ships, and had never been beaten. People said the enemy's shot just bounced off the *Constitution* and they called her "Old Ironsides." Now "Old Ironsides" was at the Academy and used as a school ship.

There were 281 midshipmen at the Academy in 1860, which was the year South Carolina left the Union. Early in 1861 midshipmen began to leave to fight for the Confederacy. The first to go was a young man from Alabama. His class gathered around him to say good-bye. They all began to sing and march past quarters and along officers' row. They made a lot of noise. When they got in front of Commandant Christopher P. R. Rodgers's quarters, he came out to ask why they were rioting on Sunday night.

They replied that they were not rioting. They were just saying good-bye to a classmate.

In a sad voice the commandant told them to continue.

This was a very hard time for Commandant Rodgers. He insisted on high ideals for his midshipmen and all his loyalty was with the North. His family had been serving the United States and the Navy ever since the country began. Three famous commodores were his uncles—John Rodgers, hero of the War of 1812; Matthew Perry, who took a fleet to Japan and opened up trade there; and Oliver Hazard Perry, who defeated the British at the Battle of Lake Erie. His brother, George Washington Rodgers, was in command of the *Constitution* while it was the school ship at the Academy. The Rodgers were a naval family. Naval families are a part of Academy tradition. Brothers follow each other into the school. Sons follow their fathers to the Academy and a career in the Navy.

Commandant Christopher P. R. Rodgers had tears in his eyes when he asked the midshipmen to be true to the flag as the Civil War began.

In April 1861, after the fighting at Fort Sumter, South Carolina, when the war really began, Superintendent Blake wrote to the Secretary of the Navy, Gideon Welles. He wrote he did not think the very young students could defend the school or the *Constitution*. He wanted to sail the ship and midshipmen to New York or Philadelphia. Secretary Welles wired back that Superintendent Blake was to save the *Constitution* at all costs. If this could not be done, he was to sink her.

Just about this time, General Benjamin F. Butler, in command of the Eighth Massachusetts Infantry, sailed down the Chesapeake Bay. He was headed for Annapolis, where he intended to disembark and lead his troops to Washington, D.C. Lieutenant G. W. Rodgers on the *Constitution* hailed Butler's ship, asking what was the ship's name.

Back came a reply. Then, "Ship ahoy, keep off, or I will sink you."

Rodgers soon learned Butler was a friend. Everyone breathed a sigh of relief.

Superintendent Blake knew the *Constitution* would be saved. Now he was concerned because the Seventh New York Regiment had arrived. Its men and Butler's men were camped all over the Yard. They were turning it into an army depot. Upper classmen gave up their rooms to officers of the regiments. The Academy Yard and buildings were just not large enough for the school and for soldiers. Superintendent Blake wrote for permission to move to Newport, Rhode Island.

Midshipmen were to sail to Newport on the *Constitution*. Before they embarked, the whole battalion met for the last time. The recently formed Academy band played "Hail Columbia" and the "Star Spangled Banner." Commandant Rodgers wanted to speak to the men about loyalty. He raised his arm and pointed to the flag and asked them all to be true to it. Tears filled his eyes and he could say no more. Some left to be true to a new flag, the stars and bars of the South. The rest sailed north and remained true to the old flag. Fourteen days later they arrived in Newport and in four days classes began at the new home.

The Seventh Regiment landing at the Naval Academy. Superintendent
Blake was worried because the soldiers were all over the
Yard and using the buildings.

Superintendent Blake had picked Newport for the school because it was an old seafaring and shipbuilding town. It was far from the South and had an empty army post, Fort Adams, that could be used. However, it soon was decided that the fort's buildings were too old and run-down to be used. The Navy rented a large hotel, the Atlantic House, in downtown Newport. It faced Touro Park, which the midshipmen used as the yard. Officer quarters and the mess hall were on the first floor. Classes were held on the second. Students lived on the third and fourth floors.

Fourth classmen and some third classmen lived and studied on the *Constitution*. Later on, it was joined by the wooden frigate *Santee*. Life on these ships was terrible. They were ice-cold in winter and boiling hot in summer. The students slept on narrow hammocks. There were no bathtubs or showers. Young men stood in lines to get a small bowl of water to clean themselves. Their food was awful. They ate it on the dark berth deck, the third deck down, which was lit by a few smoking oil lamps.

They studied at long tables on the gun deck. The gun deck was the second deck down. The only light came from some portholes or air vents in the ceiling. In a drawing of the gun deck it looks as if one midshipman at the end of a table is getting his hair cut. Perhaps the gun deck had many uses.

The midshipmen were awakened at 6:00 a.m., when they lashed their hammocks and carried them up to the top or spar deck. Then they had to climb the ropes of the sails no matter what the weather was like. They climbed to the masthead and down for exercise. When one young student protested about the lack of comfort, his officer wondered what fool ever joined the Navy to be comfortable.

Life at Newport was very dreary. There was no athletic program to give the midshipmen a chance to play. Officers and the good teachers left to go to war. Commandant Rodgers left and the battalion of midshipmen had a series of commandants after him. Soon most of the teachers were civilians, not navy men. Many of the upper class-

Members of the class of 1864 in front of the Atlantic House, Newport. Life there wasn't as strict as at the school in Annapolis. They could lounge and wear sloppy uniforms to have their picture taken.

men left to join the U.S. Navy. New classes became larger than the whole battalion had been a few years before. The Navy wanted to train as many men as quickly as possible to fight in the war.

Bright students found they didn't have to study much to pass their exams. One of them, Charles Sigsbee, said he only had to study about forty-five minutes a day. He had his picture taken as a carefree student in his lounging robe, sleep cap, and slippers. It shows how easy study was.

The Academy did its best to keep up its high standards. Summer cruises were an exciting time. The sloops *John Adams* and *Marion* sailed along the Atlantic Coast. It was always possible that one of the ships would meet a Confederate raider. They had orders to overtake and identify every ship they met. The *John Adams* visited Union bases at Yorktown, Virginia, and Port Royal, South Carolina, and gave the midshipmen an idea of army life.

The *Marion* was captained by Lieutenant Commander Stephen B. Luce. Luce had joined the Navy when he was only fourteen years old. He went to the Naval School when he was twenty-one. He had his picture made in his white sailor pants, navy jacket, and straw hat.

He became a teacher at the Academy and was made head of the Department of Seamanship. He wrote the book on seamanship that was used for the next forty years. In 1863 he commanded the *Macedonian*, which took the midshipmen on a summer cruise across the Atlantic Ocean. The next year the *Macedonian* was joined by the *Marion*, the *American*, and the steam gunboat *Marblehead*. They cruised as a squadron. This was the first time the Academy's training ships had sailed together. It gave the midshipmen training on sailing ships as well as on a new steam-driven vessel.

Some time during the four years the Academy was at Newport, classmen started hazing the plebes. Hazing is making someone do something they don't want to do, over and over again. Sometimes it is very silly, like having a plebe climb a tree, sit on a limb, and bark like a dog for hours. Sometimes it is very cruel. Thomas G. Welles,

Studying at the long table on the cold gun deck of the *Constitution*.

Midshipman Charles Sigsbee in sleep cap, robe, and slippers, to show
how easy studying was at Newport.

son of the Secretary of the Navy, was hazed by being thrown over-board the *Santee*. Then he was dragged back and forth by a rope tied around his waist. He was so upset by this experience that he resigned from the Navy.

The officers of the school forbade hazing. When he was superintendent after the War Between the States, Rear Admiral Christopher P. R. Rodgers tried to stop it. Many other superintendents tried to stop it, but midshipmen kept right on doing it. Jimmy Carter, the only Academy graduate to become president of the United States, said that hazing was a rough part of his years there.

Finally on April 9, 1865, the terrible Civil War was over. There were 659 graduates at the end of the war. Ninety-five of them had served in the Confederate Navy. Because of this, they lost their commissions in the U.S. Navy and had to find other ways to earn their livings. Superintendent Buchanan became a professor at another school.

Superintendent Blake had saved the *Constitution* and held the Academy together. Now he was ready to move the school back to Annapolis. Newport and many other places tried to get Secretary Welles to move the Academy to one of their towns. He held fast for Annapolis. Then Congress passed an act that said Annapolis, Maryland, always was to be the Academy's home.

The *Constitution*—"Old Ironsides"—as it might have looked sailing the
midshipmen back to Annapolis from Newport.

# A Time for Growth

The midshipmen sailed back to Annapolis on board the *Constitution*. She was towed by tugboats out of the Newport harbor. Then she was turned loose, her sails were unfurled, and she raced down the Atlantic Coast at 13 1/2 knots. This is about 15 miles per hour. It was great speed in the year 1865. She was a beautiful sight racing along.

The trip proved that Academy men got good seamanship training while they were at Newport. This was due to the teaching of Lieutenant Commander Luce, who had taken them on summer cruises and written their textbook. It also proved that "Old Ironsides" was a ship of which to be proud. She stayed at the Academy until 1871. She was used as quarters for the incoming class and as a training ship. Now she is berthed in Boston, Massachusetts.

When the *Constitution* docked at Annapolis, the midshipmen, officers, and teachers could not believe what they saw. The Academy and Yard were a wreck. Regiments of soldiers had camped there. The Army had had a hospital on the grounds and had put up a lot of tents. The buildings had been used for all sorts of things. The superintendent's house was used as a billiard parlor. The grass and bushes were gone from the Yard. Most of the trees were gone. Army wagons had criss-crossed the Yard and left deep ruts everywhere. There were foot paths and trash all over the place.

The Academy needed someone to fix everything. It needed someone to get officers to come back to teach. It needed someone to make sure there were good courses in gunnery and seamanship. On September 9, 1865, Rear Admiral David Dixon Porter, just the man to do all this, was appointed the new superintendent.

Porter had been in the Navy most of his life. His father was Commander David Porter, who had fought pirates in the Caribbean, won important battles in his ship *Essex* in the War of 1812, and even was an admiral in charge of the Mexican Navy. When he was only eleven years old, Superintendent Porter fought pirate ships in the West Indies. He was in the Mexican Navy when his father was its admiral. When the Civil War began, he was a lieutenant in the U.S. Navy. Two years later he was a rear admiral! He was a man who knew how to get things done.

The first thing he did was to hire a lot of men to clean up the Yard. When classes started again in October 1865, the Academy almost was ship-shape. The grounds still needed a lot of planting, especially new trees. Porter felt they needed new buildings and land, too. The school was a small place. It had started twenty years ago with only nine acres and the buildings of Fort Severn. Now it had over one hundred acres and sixteen more buildings.

Superintendent Porter wanted to make the Academy a school that would rival West Point. He was able to get the Congress to give the Navy money for more land and buildings. He bought four acres right outside the gate where there was a beautiful garden. This land went down to the harbor and on it was the home of the Maryland governors. Porter used it for the library and the superintendent's offices.

He bought ten acres of land from St. John's College, which was nearby. Next he bought the sixty-seven acres across College Creek called Strawberry Hill and built a hospital there. He also laid out the Naval Academy Cemetery.

Rear Admiral David Dixon Porter—just the man to fix up the
Naval Academy after the Civil War.

His most important building was called "New Quarters." Even after it was old, it was called this. New Quarters was a long, red brick building with a cupola on top. It had an iron porch along its 203-foot length. The midshipmen lived on the upper floors. There was running water inside this new dorm and midshipmen were ordered to take a bath once a week. Their mess hall and classrooms were on the ground floor. All the upper classmen lived there. The plebe class lived on the *Constitution* just as they had in Newport.

There were almost six hundred students now and Superintendent Porter wanted them to have the best education possible. He got in touch with many of the navy people to help him find bright young officers to be teachers. He was able to dismiss a lot of the teachers who were not navy men. These were the ones who had taught at Newport when most of the officers were at war. He arranged for Lieutenant Commander Luce to come back as commandant of the midshipmen. The men he chose to teach gunnery, navigation, and physics all became superintendents of the Academy at later dates.

Some of the courses and the way subjects were taught were changed. The students did more than just recite lessons. They practiced gunnery from the *Santee* and rattled windows in nearby buildings. They practiced seamanship with working models of sailing ships. They held sail drill on practice ships anchored in the Severn. They had courses in steam engineering, which they did not like. To show the students how much better steam vessels were than sailing ones, Porter and the Chief Engineer decided to turn a steam launch into a brig. Sad to say, on the trial voyage when the boat's boiler was fired, it exploded and killed everyone. Luckily for Porter, he was sick that day and did not go on the cruise so was not on board when the dreadful accident happened.

One of the most important things at the Academy is the "Navy Spirit." This is what gives midshipmen pride in the Navy and teaches them to have self-control. Superintendent Porter knew it didn't come just from study. He restored discipline. Students got demerits if they

Midshipmen posing in front of the fancy iron porch of their
"New Quarters."

Midshipmen lounging in their room in the modern New Quarters that
even had running water and gas lighting.

Midshipmen practiced seamanship with working models of sailing ships.

did not obey orders, but he let them work off the demerits by doing guard duty. He started the honor system. Students were not spied upon and what they told an officer was regarded as the truth.

Up until now, the midshipmen had no organized athletic program. Now there was a change. Shooting galleries and bowling alleys were built on the first floor of Fort Severn. The second floor was changed into a gymnasium. Boxing lessons were given to the first class. Porter went one round with a midshipman but he got punched in the nose. The different classes started baseball teams and rugby teams and formed rowing crews. Porter was a great supporter of all the teams. He told the students he didn't want any other school coming and beating them at anything.

The Academy was being turned into a first-rate school, but there was more to come. The battalions were organized into four divisions. A marine detachment came to take part in parades and ceremonies. The midshipmen's uniforms were changed. Now they had a stand-up collar with an anchor on each side. Today their dress uniforms still look like this.

There were other changes. Balls were held and musical clubs formed. The officers' wives invited upper classmen to tea. There were minstrel shows and plays where the midshipmen acted the parts of women. All of these activities added to the spirit of the school. The old sailors who had been against starting the Academy thought they were frills. They called the school "Porter's Dancing Academy."

President Ulysses S. Grant came to make the graduation speech in 1869. This was the first time a president of the United States had done this. Many presidents have spoken at graduation since then. President Grant saw the fine work David Dixon Porter had done and asked him to take over the Navy Department and improve it.

After Porter left, there were twelve different superintendents between 1869 and 1906. Some of them were very good and some were not. Rear Admiral Rodgers, who had asked everyone to be true to the flag when the Civil War began, came back twice to help the

Midshipmen in 1888 in the uniforms of different sports—football,
tennis, baseball, fencing, rifle.

Academy. He was interested in courses in steam engineering. Congress had approved the appointment of twenty-four cadet engineers to a four-year course. Rodgers added boiler-making, blacksmithing, and engine-building courses. He made the Academy the first school to offer a course in mechanical engineering. A small fleet of steam launches was added to train the midshipmen. At the Paris Universal Exposition of 1878, the Academy received a gold medal for the best system of education in the United States. This honor was due to the work of Superintendent Rodgers.

There were other changes, too. In 1872 James Conyers became the first black midshipman. He was the plebe who was hazed by being made to sit in the top of a tree and bark like a dog. There was an uproar over this as he was wearing only his nightshirt and it was winter. Several other African Americans entered the Academy but they didn't stay to graduate, mostly because of mistreatment like this. Conyers didn't graduate either, and it wasn't until 1949 that the first African American graduated from the Academy. His name was Wesley A. Brown.

Other improvements took a long time as the United States was not interested in a navy now that the Civil War was over. Five years after the end of the war the U.S. Navy was one of the smallest in the world. Midshipmen who graduated had little chance of getting any kind of sea duty. There were not enough ships for them to sail on. They had little chance for promotion.

Finally in 1883 the Congress voted money to build three cruisers and one dispatch boat. Three years later it gave funds for the steel battleships, the *Maine* and the *Texas.*

In 1883, when the size of the Navy began to grow, the Academy had one of its worst times. Cadet Petty Officer Charles E. Woodruff put the answers to a math test on the inside of a hall door. He wanted to help his classmates pass the exam. One of the strongest parts of the Academy's honor system is to never, ever show test answers to anyone. Captain Francis M. Ramsey was superintendent

At "Porter's Dancing Academy," midshipmen dressed as women to act parts in plays. Twenty years later in 1885 they were still doing it.

then. He took away Woodruff's rank. Then he did the same to Cadet Lieutenant George W. Street as he led the midshipmen in the mess hall in a cheer for Woodruff. The midshipmen hissed and laughed when they heard what Superintendent Ramsey had done. Ramsey had the entire first class marched to the old frigate *Santee*. It was now used as the prison ship for midshipmen being punished for not obeying orders. All the other classes were put on restriction. The midshipmen made fun of the superintendent by calling the school "Ramsey's Kindergarten," but his actions restored discipline and order. A year later Ramsey was able to commend the class that he had punished on the *Santee*.

On February 2, 1898, the pride of the Navy, the new steel battleship *Maine,* blew up in Havana harbor, Cuba. It had been sent there to protect Americans who lived in Cuba. Spain ruled the land, but the Cubans were rebelling against this rule. The United States did not want any Americans involved in a fight.

Americans could not believe the news that the ship was destroyed. They blamed the Spanish. Today it is believed it was an internal explosion, but Americans shouted the slogan, "Remember the *Maine.*" Congress declared war on Spain. Two Academy graduates, Commander William T. Sampson and Lieutenant Commander Winfield Scott Schley, were sent in command of squadrons to defeat the Spanish in Cuba. Rear Admiral Pascual Cervera y Topete commanded the Spanish Fleet at Santiago, Cuba. When he tried to sail his squadron to safety, he was attacked and quickly defeated by the Americans on July 3, 1898.

Cervera y Topete and his officers were sent to the Naval Academy to be held as prisoners. Many of them were put in the New Quarters. Although they were prisoners of war, they were allowed to roam the Yard and go into Annapolis. The Spanish were so polite and dignified that everyone admired them. Ladies even asked them to autograph their fans. They were sent home in a few months.

Earlier, in May, Admiral George Dewey had defeated the Spanish

*Top*, midshipmen training on the small steam launches and making lots of smoke. The *Santee* is in the background. It has a roof on it and looks like it did when Superintendent Ramsey had the first class marched there to be put in prison.

*Below*, Battle in Santiago Harbor, Cuba, where two Academy graduates, William T. Sampson and Winfield Scott Schley, defeated the Spanish under Rear Admiral Cervera y Topete.

in the Philippines. Dewey was a Naval Academy graduate. In fact the Spanish-American War was the first war in which Academy graduates held all the chief commands. The fame of the U.S. Navy was beginning to grow; so was the fame and size of the Naval Academy.

# Mr. Flagg Designs a New Yard

In 1895 the Academy's Board of Visitors decided that the school needed all new buildings. They hired Ernest Flagg, a well-known New York architect who had studied in France, to make a whole new plan for the Academy. The U.S. Congress voted the huge sum of $1,000,000 for this project. Flagg decided to get rid of all the old buildings that had been put here, there, and everywhere in the Yard. He designed huge granite buildings to be placed around three sides of a square. The fourth side, which faced the Severn River, was left open to the water. Flagg's buildings gave the Academy the look of a large, modern college. They are all still there in the Yard. There are newer buildings, too. Flagg kept plenty of room in his plan for the Academy to grow. Over the years more room has been made by landfills along the water.

The old buildings were torn down one by one as the work on Flagg's design went on. The only remaining old buildings are the two guardhouses at Gate 3 on Maryland Avenue. Even old Fort Severn was torn down although many people tried to save it. It was the last of the buildings of the Naval School of 1845 to vanish.

Part of Flagg's plan included a huge new dormitory that could house 460 midshipmen. Part of it was opened in 1904. It was named

The Naval Academy with Ernest Flagg's huge new buildings,
including Bancroft Hall. Tiny Fort Severn is in front of it.

The chapel dome and gold spire can be seen from everywhere in the Yard.

From left to right: Colonel Robert M. Thompson; Evelyn B.
Longman, who designed doors for the new chapel; Ernest Flagg, architect
of the chapel.
The bronze doors Evelyn B. Longman designed, showing peace on one
panel and war on the other.

Bancroft Hall to honor the man who started the academy, Secretary of the Navy George Bancroft.

Today Bancroft Hall has room for over four thousand midshipmen. It has a huge curved roof mess, King Hall, that can seat them all at once. Its galleys can serve a meal to everyone in less than one hour. A store, bank, post office, dentist, barber, sick bay, and tailor are all in the building so the midshipmen have everything they need in one building. Over the years eight wings have been added to Bancroft Hall. They are connected by five miles of hallways. The building is joined by covered walks to Macdonough and Dahlgren halls.

Bancroft Hall is a massive building adorned with many windows and sculptures. Up a wide marble flight of stairs from the marble-floored entrance hall is beautiful Memorial Hall. It has sparkling crystal chandeliers and paintings of famous naval scenes. There are bronze tablets along the walls in memory of Academy men who lost their lives in the course of duty. Midshipmen feel it is a hallowed place.

In the same year that Bancroft Hall opened, Admiral Dewey laid the cornerstone for the new chapel, saying he declared the stone well and truly laid. The chapel is in the central part of Flagg's plan and faces the Severn River. Its large copper-covered dome with a gold spire can be seen from any spot in the Yard.

The Academy held a contest for the best design of doors for the new chapel. To everyone's surprise, Evelyn B. Longman won. She was only nineteen years old but already was known as a good sculptress. It was the first time a woman's work was recognized by the Academy. The bronze doors Evelyn Longman sculpted show peace on one panel and war on the other.

The chapel is the final resting place of John Paul Jones. After the Revolutionary War, Jones went abroad. He died a poor man in France. Many years later, in 1905, Horace Porter, the American ambassador to France, found Jones's grave in Paris. His body was in a lead coffin full of spirits; so it was well preserved and that's how they knew it was John Paul Jones.

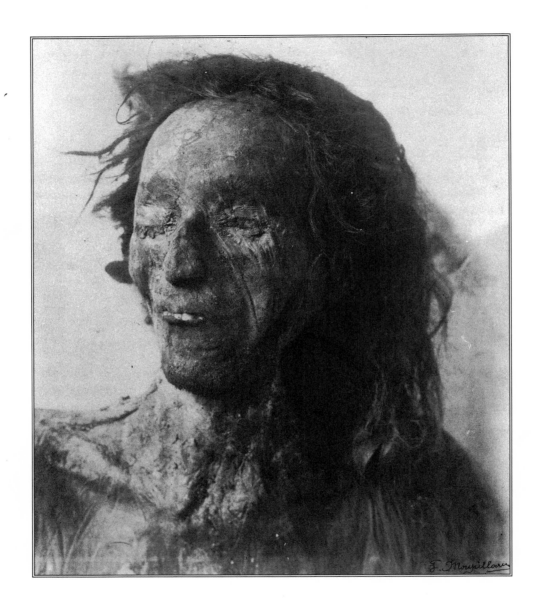

John Paul Jones's corpse as it looked when Ambassador Porter
found it in France.

John Paul Jones's crypt in the chapel.

Theodore Roosevelt was the president then. He believed in a strong navy. He got Congress to vote funds for ships year after year. He felt that bringing Jones home would be good for the sailors' and midshipmen's spirits. He sent a whole squadron of ships to escort the coffin home. It was brought to Dahlgren Hall, next to Bancroft Hall. On April 26, 1906, there was a large ceremony to honor the hero; Roosevelt gave the main talk.

Roosevelt got Congress to vote funds to build a special room called a crypt for the coffin. The crypt where John Paul Jones is laid to rest is in the basement of the chapel. His green marble sarcophagus, which contains his coffin, is surrounded by gold stars and, also in gold, the names of his ships and the ships he fought at sea. You can visit the crypt when you tour the Academy.

The middle part of Ernest Flagg's plan is now a restful space of big trees and green grass. Wide brick walkways running from Mahan Hall to Bancroft Hall are known as Stribling Walk. They are where the row of buildings called Stribling Row was when the Academy was new. Park benches along the walks are a good place to sit and think about the Academy's famous monuments.

The Academy's oldest monument is the Herndon Monument across from the chapel. It is a granite shaft put there in 1859 to honor the memory of Commander William Louis Herndon. He went down with his mail boat, the *Central America,* in a storm off Cape Hatteras, North Carolina. When Herndon realized he could not save his ship, he went below and put on his full dress uniform. Then he stood at attention on the deck as he and the ship went down to their watery graves.

The plebe class turns the monument into a test of endurance every year to celebrate the end of their first year. A sailor's hat is put on top of the shaft and they try to climb up to get it. That sounds easy, but first the shaft is greased with a lot of lard and motor oil. Then the plebes slip and slide and push and shove until someone finally gets the hat.

Slipping and shoving and pushing to climb Herndon and get the hat.

Tecumseh, the best-known figure in the Yard, faces Tecumseh Court in front of Bancroft Hall. Tecumseh was carved in 1820 as the wooden figurehead of the ship *Delaware*. He was a model of Tamanend, a friendly chief of the Delaware Indians. In 1861, at the start of the Civil War, the U.S. Navy destroyed the fleet anchored at the Norfolk, Virginia, Navy Yard. They didn't want the South to get the ships. The *Delaware* was one of them and was sunk. Someone saved the figurehead and brought it to Annapolis.

Midshipmen gave him the nickname "Tecumseh." They felt he could bring them luck. They put him in the Yard so they could throw good-luck pennies at him every day. Poor wooden Tecumseh. He showed signs of wear after years of being outside. They made a metal copy of him that they put in the Yard facing Bancroft Hall. They put the wooden Tecumseh safely inside Halsey Field House. Today if mids are bilging (bilging means failing a course), they throw pennies at the metal Tecumseh to bring them luck. For luck they paint the metal and the wooden figureheads before each Army-Navy football game. His eyes are painted blue and gold, and blue and gold stripes run down his cheeks. These are the Academy's colors.

The Academy's museum is in Preble Hall. The museum began the same time as the school did, in 1845. Then it was called the Naval School Lyceum. President James K. Polk in 1849 ordered that all the Navy's famous battle flags be sent to the lyceum. One of the most famous is dark blue with big white letters—DON'T GIVE UP THE SHIP. It is the flag Oliver H. Perry flew during the Battle of Lake Erie in the War of 1812. The words had been said over and over again just a few months before, by young James Lawrence as he was dying on his ship, the *Chesapeake*. Lawrence's words and Perry's flag are two of the Navy's hallowed symbols. You can see the flag in Memorial Hall, a part of Bancroft Hall.

More and more things were added to the lyceum. In 1930 Preble Hall was built to be the U.S. Naval Academy Museum. There is much to see, cannons, swords, flags, ship models, paintings, and photographs.

Tecumseh, painted with blue and gold stripes for good luck before an Army-Navy football game.

It has everything, from a large collection of medals to the long dresses and big hats worn by color girls during June Week. You can spend a lot of time there when you visit the Academy.

One of the displays shows cartoons from *Shakings,* a book made by Park Benjamin of the class of 1867. Benjamin filled the book with funny drawings of life at the school. In one of them the students at gun drill are standing around holding their ears. Another shows the men on fire room watch roasting potatoes in the furnaces.

Benjamin also designed the Academy's coat of arms. You can see it above the main door of Bancroft Hall and in many other places. It shows an ancient sailing galley in full sail. Below it is an open book. Above it Neptune's hand is holding a trident. The carved motto, "Ex Scientia, Tridens," means in Latin that sea power comes from knowledge. It was adopted as the official seal of the Naval Academy in 1898.

Roasting potatoes while on fire room watch, Park Benjamin's drawing.

*Top*, an early football team with their stocking caps and laced vests.
*Bottom*, a group of midshipmen cheering at an early football game.

# The Academy Gets a Goat
## and a Tune

After Superintendent Porter introduced athletics as part of the curriculum, sports were introduced to the Academy one by one. One of the first was fencing, taught by Swordmaster Antoine J. Corborsier, who came in 1865. For forty years he introduced midshipmen to the use of sword, cutlass, and epee. He also drilled them in the manual of arms.

Baseball was added in 1873, then crew and football. By the time Ernest Flagg's new buildings were getting started, the Academy had four varsity sports. Today when you visit the Sports Hall of Fame in Lejeune Hall you can see awards given to athletes in over thirty-three sports. Some of the ones most people don't think of are water polo, track, tennis, squash, lacrosse, and rifle.

Sometimes a sport was interrupted for a few years. In 1877 the Navy crew rowed against the University of Pennsylvania and lost. Just after this a gale with strong winds and high water destroyed the boathouse and fifteen shells. There was no crew again for ten years.

Army-Navy football games were also suspended for a period of five years. This happened after a game when a rear admiral and a brigadier general came to blows and challenged each other to a duel at the Army-Navy Club in Washington, D.C. The Secretary of the

Sports at the Academy.
Bill the Goat and the football team ready to "Beat Army."

Push-ups, pull-ups, and sit-ups, known as "Applied Struggle."

Army and the Secretary of the Navy did not like this and canceled the games.

Of course football, and the exciting Army-Navy game, is the sport by which the Academy is best known. Football started in 1879. Then it was really a kind of soccer. The first game was played against the Baltimore Athletic Club in the superintendent's cow pasture. Before the game midshipmen went to Bellis, the tailor, and had him make a sleeveless jacket of canvas. It was laced to tightly fit the chest. They felt that if it got wet with sweat or rain it would be hard to grab onto. They knew about wet canvas from drilling with sails.

One game was played on November 28, 1882, in the snow, against Johns Hopkins University. The kick-off was at 10:30 in the morning. During the first hour the ball was kicked over the sea wall and the game delayed until someone rowed out to get the ball out of the water. In spite of this setback, Navy won by two touchdowns. Hopkins had none.

In 1890 the football team traveled to West Point for the first Army-Navy game. They wore the canvas vests, red and white striped stocking caps, and red stockings. The famous colors of Navy Blue and Old Gold were not used until two years later. During the game Navy dropped back to kick and instead ran for a touchdown. Such a trick play was unheard of and Army felt it was a false thing for an officer and a gentleman to do!

It was during this game the midshipmen thought of having a mascot for their team. On the way to West Point they talked about Yale's bulldog mascot, "Handsome Dan." Spying an old goat grazing in a yard, they grabbed it for their good luck mascot. It must have worked because Navy won 24-0. In the Sports Hall of Fame there is a gold football that has the following lettered on it: "West Point, NY-November 29, 1890, Navy 24-Army 0." There is a gold football for each Army-Navy game that the Navy has won with the place, date, and score. In 1906 Bill the Goat, although not the original goat, was made the team's official mascot.

Robert Means Thompson had graduated in the class of 1868. He resigned his commission and made a lot of money in business. Then he used his money to help the Academy. He was the man who got Ernest Flagg to redesign the Yard. In 1890 he told the alumni that the Academy must turn out officers with strong nerves and healthy bodies. He felt athletics were necessary to do this and helped found the Naval Academy Athletic Association in 1891. He donated a huge silver cup that is given every year to the top athlete in the Academy.

Athletics and physical training are an important part of a midshipman's daily life. Everyone must be part of some sport every season, every year they are at the Academy. There are many places for them to do this. There is the Halsey Field House for indoor track, a pool for water polo in Macdonough Hall, an ice hockey rink in Dahlgren Hall, and olympic and diving pools in Lejeune Hall.

Different fields for different sports are named for naval heroes, among them Dewey Field and Farragut Field. There are outdoor tracks, bowling alleys, boxing rings, tennis and squash courts, rowing shells, sailboats, and many other facilities. Each midshipman must pass a swimming test every year and another test that is full of push-ups, pull-ups, and sit-ups and known in their slang as "Applied Struggle."

Over the years the midshipmen have engaged in other activities. One of the most important is music. The best-known music from the Academy is the stirring tune "Anchor's Aweigh." It is played every time Navy scores a touchdown during football games. It is played when the Navy marches anywhere. Lieutenant Charles Adam Zimmerman composed "Anchor's Aweigh" and it was first played at the Army-Navy game of 1906.

Zimmerman had joined the first Academy band, which was made up of civilians. Every year he wrote a new march for each graduating class, which gave him a medal for it. He proudly wore these on his uniform. When the band became part of the Navy Department, Zimmerman was made its leader and did a lot to make music an important part of the school.

Charles Adam Zimmerman, composer of "Anchor's Aweigh,"
with his many medals, one for every new march.

Midshipmen also began different publications. In 1894, *Lucky Bag*, the yearbook, was started. Of course, *Lucky Bag* has pictures of all the graduating members of the first class. It also lists their home towns and highlights of the year. A yearly manual for plebes called *Reef Points* was begun in 1906. Plebes are the freshmen. It tells entering midshipmen all they need to know about the Academy. *Reef Points* includes a long list of Academy slang that a plebe must learn. These are words devised by midshipmen—"Mrs. Supe" for the superintendent's wife; "You're down" for you are in deep trouble; "Wooley Pulley" for a black sweater. They also publish *The Log*, a monthly humor magazine, and *The Trident*, a weekly paper full of local naval news, pictures, and calendar of events.

Traditional events are an important part of academy life. The most traditional event of the year is Commissioning Week, once known as June Week. This is when the first classmen graduate; many of the rituals go back a long time. One of them, the Color Parade, was begun in 1890. The colors are the flags. It is a high honor to be in the color guard and carry one of them—the Stars and Stripes, the Navy flag, the Marine flag, and the Academy flag. At the Color Parade the date or a friend of the commander of the best-drilled company accepts the Academy's colors from the superintendent. Then he or she gives them to the commander of the company that earned the most points for studies, athletics, parades, and military performance during the year. Members of that company wear a gold "E" for excellence on their uniforms.

The Ring Dance is another long-established custom of the week. Second classmen can put on their class rings after the last exam of the year. At one time this was celebrated when the first classmen dragged the second classmen to Dewey Basin and tossed them into the Severn River. Sad to say, in 1924 one of the midshipmen hit his head and drowned. They stopped tossing each other into the river. Instead the second classmen and their dates walk through a big model of the ring. Before putting their rings on their fingers, the midshipmen dip the rings in a basin full of water from the seven seas.

The color guard in front of Bancroft Hall.

Second classmen and their dates ready to walk through the huge ring
models during the June Week Ring Dance, 1957.

Commissioning Week opens with the Dedication Parade, which honors the faculty of the Academy. Next comes the event simply known as "Herndon," when the plebes try to climb the greased Herndon Monument.

The week ends, of course, with graduation—the event everyone has worked toward for the past four years. After the ceremonies, after the speeches, after the awarding of degrees, the first classmen whoop with joy. Now they are either ensigns in the U.S. Navy or second lieutenants in the U.S. Marine Corps. They jump up, yell, and toss their white hats high in the air. This tradition started with the class of 1911 and the sky has been full of white hats ever since on graduation day.

A sky full of hats on Graduation Day.

# Honorable Service and
# Brave Deeds

(O)ne of the new buildings Ernest Flagg designed is Mahan Hall. It is named for Rear Admiral Alfred Thayer Mahan, an early Academy graduate. Mahan taught at the Naval War College. He spent his life teaching and writing about the history of sea power. A navy that is powerful has strong officers. Mahan wrote that a good naval officer has self-control, stays calm when everyone else is excited, obeys the law, and is not afraid to try new ways to do things. Many graduates have shown that the Naval Academy taught them all the things Mahan wrote about.

One of them was Lieutenant John Rodgers, whose Maryland family had served the Navy for generations. In 1903 two brothers from Dayton, Ohio, Wilbur and Orville Wright, flew the first airplane with an engine. They did this on the sand dunes at Kitty Hawk, North Carolina. Their plane stayed in the air for a few seconds. This new way to travel excited a lot of people, including Rodgers. He went to the Wright Brothers aviation school in Ohio. He learned to fly and became the second naval pilot.

The Navy's first airport was built across the Severn River from the Academy. In September 1911 three pusher-type planes were delivered in crates to the airport. They did not look at all like today's airplanes. They were a metal frame with a motor, two wings, and a seat in the open air for the pilot. The three planes that came in crates were put together in one afternoon.

The next day Rodgers took off from Farragut Field. He did turns and spirals and buzzed the field and landed safely!

Rodgers remained a navy pilot and in 1925 flew a navy seaplane on a flight from San Francisco to Hawaii. Seaplanes were great clumsy things with pontoons instead of wheels so they could land in water. This was a test flight to see how far a seaplane could fly. All went well until about four hundred miles from Hawaii when the plane ran out of gas. Rodgers and his crew were adrift on the Pacific Ocean for nine days. Rodgers made a sail out of the wing fabric; in those days the wings were frames covered with canvas. This is how they stayed afloat until they were spotted by a boat and rescued only fifteen miles from shore. Even though they came down, they had set a record for the longest flight.

There is a plaque in honor of Rodgers in Bancroft Hall's Memorial Hall. It says that he dedicated his life to the advancement of aviation. He died in a flying accident in 1926.

Academy men were pioneers in sailing under the seas. A man named John P. Holland built one of the earliest submarines. His ship was at the Academy for five years. It was a small thing that could make seven knots on the surface, but couldn't go as fast under water. Below water it could only go about fifty miles before it ran out of gas. It didn't have a periscope and often had to come back up to the surface so sailors could see where they were.

Boat sailors called it a "pigboat" because it was little, crowded, and smelly. There wasn't any way to get fresh air into the submarine. Sailing in it was dangerous but many midshipmen were proud to serve in it. As the submarine developed, more and more sailors volunteered for that duty.

The little, crowded "pigboat," climbing aboard the early
submarine, in 1902.

Another pioneer was Admiral William S. Sims, who did many new things for the Navy. One of them was the convoy system he used in World War I. In 1914 Britain and France went to war against Germany. The United States helped them by sending much-needed supplies and arms across the Atlantic Ocean. The German Navy had a lot of submarines. They used them to sink these merchant ships as often as they could.

Sims, who had graduated from the Academy in 1880, was sent to England to find out if the U.S. Navy could help. Sims made a bold plan to stop the U-boat attacks; German submarines were called U-boats. Under his plan, navy ships would go with the merchant ships. The navy ships would act as protection. Many officials were afraid this would leave America's shores unprotected. Sims knew that Germany had only a few submarines that could come clear across the Atlantic. There was not much danger from them and the plan of escorting the ships worked.

Later when the United States joined the war, Sims was given command of the U.S. Fleet in Europe. Navy ships were used to escort the shiploads of soldiers going across the Atlantic Ocean to fight the Germans. It was called the convoy system. It saved many lives and helped the United States, Britain, and France win World War I. Sailors loved Sims because he was a leader who cared for their safety and treated them with consideration.

Fleet Admiral Chester A. Nimitz was another graduate who was beloved by his men. Nimitz grew up in Texas and didn't know a thing about the Naval Academy. He went there because his family was poor and the Academy was free. When he graduated in 1905, he knew that the Navy was where he wanted to be for the rest of his life. He loved ships, submarines, and sailors. He rose in rank and by December 7, 1941, was a rear admiral, chief of the Bureau of Navigation.

December 7, 1941, the day President Franklin D. Roosevelt said would live in infamy, was when the Japanese dive bombed the fleet at Pearl Harbor, Hawaii. Almost all the ships of the Pacific Fleet were

Admiral Chester W. Nimitz talking to some of his men.

*Top,* "A date which will live in infamy"—ships burning in the harbor, the sky full of flak during the Japanese attack on Pearl Harbor, December 7, 1941. *Bottom,* Lieutenant John Rodgers being pushed off to do some turns around Farragut Field.

docked there when the Japanese attacked. Eighteen ships were wrecked and 2,008 sailors were killed. It was the worst disaster ever to hit the U.S. Navy. Congress declared war.

After the attack, the Navy was able to raise all the sunken ships except the USS *Arizona*. It is still at the bottom of Pearl Harbor, where a memorial has been built to the sailors who died on that day of infamy.

Right after the Pearl Harbor attack, Nimitz was made commander of the Pacific Fleet. He arrived at Pearl Harbor on Christmas Day 1941 to see the terrible wrecks. He was known as a man who could make a quick judgment and stick to it. He believed that the country that controlled the sea would influence all the world.

Nimitz knew that the war against Japan could not be won in the old way of one ship fighting another ship. It would be fought in different seas, on different islands and different countries. It would be a huge operation. Nimitz helped plan the way to defeat Japan. He used ships, airplanes, and submarines working together in all the different places they fought. He understood his men and was considerate of them. He became known as the most beloved of all the fleet commanders in World War II.

In 1973 the Academy dedicated its large new library to Nimitz, who did so much to defeat the Japanese in World War II.

A graduate who was not beloved by his men was Admiral Hyman Rickover. He was a rude man with a short temper. He also was a genius and spent his career developing nuclear power for the Navy. In January 1955 the *Nautilus*, the first nuclear-powered submarine, was launched. The nuclear-powered submarine could do many things the old subs could not do. It could stay under water forever. It could shoot torpedoes under water for long distances. Its torpedoes hit their targets almost every time.

Rickover expected everyone to do their very best work every minute of every day. President Jimmy Carter, the only Academy graduate to become president of the United States, learned this early in his naval career.

James Earl Carter, known as Jimmy, attended officer's training school for submarine duty in 1948 after he had graduated. He became very interested in the idea of nuclear power and decided to apply for Rickover's program. He had an interview with Rickover that he never forgot.

During the interview the admiral let Carter choose what he wanted to talk about. Of course he picked subjects that he knew a lot about. He felt the interview was going well when suddenly the admiral asked him if he had done his very best while studying at Annapolis. Carter answered truthfully that he had not always done his very best. Rickover asked, "Why not?" and the interview was over.

Many years later when he was running to be president, Carter wrote an autobiography that he titled "Why Not the Best?" He believed it was a good motto for all Americans.

It is very hard for a person to do their very best when they are a prisoner of war. James B. Stockdale, who graduated in 1947, proved that is the time when a person must do their best every day. Stockdale was a pilot in the Vietnamese War. He was shot down and taken prisoner in 1964. He stayed a prisoner for seven bad, long years. The years were full of torture, isolation, beatings, hunger.

Stockdale kept his hope during all those years. He did his best to live through each terrible day. As senior officer in a group of prisoners, he worked very hard to see that the men kept their self-discipline and their pride. His constant courage set an example for everyone.

When the war was over and Stockdale came home, he stayed in the Navy. He was awarded the Medal of Honor and promoted to vice admiral. He became a member of the Academic Advisory Board of the Academy.

Academy men were pioneers in flying and submarine work. They also were pioneers in space travel. In 1958 the United States started a new agency called the National Aeronautics and Space Administration. It became known as NASA. It started Project Mercury to put a man into space.

President Jimmy Carter and Admiral Hyman G. Rickover speaking to a
group at the USS *Los Angeles,* a nuclear-powered submarine.
A painting of a nuclear submarine shooting a torpedo.

President Jimmy Carter visiting Bancroft Hall during June Week. Maybe
he told the young midshipmen to always do their best.

There was a graduate just waiting for this. His name was Alan B. Shepard, Jr., and he had been interested in flying ever since he was a boy. He was a navy pilot during the Korean War. After that he was a test pilot. He had flown many kinds of planes. NASA sent letters to one hundred and ten pilots asking them to apply for Project Mercury. Shepard applied at once.

After a test and medical check-ups, seven men were chosen for the project. Shepard was one of them. The seven men then went through two years of training. Only one man could be chosen for the first flight into space. Shepard was the one chosen. He named his space capsule "Freedom 7" and on May 5, 1961, made his historic flight.

Later on, he flew to the moon with Edgar Mitchell and Stuart Roosa in Apollo 14. After that flight he became the first astronaut promoted to admiral in the U.S. Navy.

During the years from Lieutenant John Rodgers's first flight until after Lieutenant Shepard walked on the moon, the Academy kept on growing. Classes were changed and new classes added. More leave was given during the year. In the old days the midshipmen only got off on Christmas Day. They get a longer Christmas leave now. They still get demerits for talking in ranks, being late, or frenching (skipping over the wall to town without permission).

The Yard grew, too. New buildings filled the open spaces in Flagg's plan. They were often named for Academy men: Chauvenet Hall for the head of the Old Philadelphia Naval Asylum; Halsey Field House for graduate Admiral William "Bull" Halsey, famous in World War II. Old buildings were torn down to make room for the big new Alumni Hall, which has a modern theater. A new visitors' center, Ricketts Hall, was built next to the Halsey Field House. When you go to the Academy, Ricketts Hall should be your first stop. There you can get a map and join a guided tour of the Yard.

Midshipmen of the class of 1972 present Alan Shepard with
an award that includes a picture of his moon walk and
the official seal of the Naval Academy.

# To Be a Midshipman

When Secretary of the Navy George Bancroft began the Naval School in 1845, he did not think of letting women become students. No one had ever heard of a woman sailor or midshipman. It took a long time for people to think about women becoming midshipmen. One hundred and thirty years after the Academy began, President Gerald Ford signed the bill that said women could go to the Academy. On July 9, 1976, eighty-one women became members of the incoming class of plebes.

Today you can see women everywhere at the Academy. In the summer one of them might be training a squad of plebes. The squad will have men and women of all races in it. They come to the Academy in the summer and begin very hard training. They chant answers to the leader's questions as they march about the Yard. They do physical exercises including a lot of push ups.

Plebes get their hair all cut off the first day they are at the Academy. They wear a white sailor suit with a white sailor hat. They are allowed to have a watch, an alarm clock, snapshots, and not much else. They are not allowed to have radios, CDs, TVs, or cars. Plebe year is a very tough time. It is no wonder that in May, when their

Training the plebes during the summer.

plebe year is over, they celebrate by climbing Herndon. Then they become youngsters, or third classmen.

Youngsters help the new plebes learn about the Academy's way of doing things. Second classmen, who are juniors, train the plebes. First classmen run the companies and help with running the brigade.

The brigade is the name for all the midshipmen together, and is called the Brigade of Midshipmen. It has regiments, battalions, and companies. Each company has about one hundred and twenty midshipmen. They all live in the same part of Bancroft Hall for two years. Then the companies are mixed up. The midshipmen are changed from one company to another and live in a different part of Bancroft Hall.

All the midshipmen wear uniforms whenever they are in the Yard. There are different kinds of uniforms. The easiest thing to remember is that in the summer the uniform can be white. In the winter it is always black, but they call it "navy blue." There are working uniforms and full dress uniforms. Insignia on the uniforms tell what class the midshipman is in and what his or her rank is. You can tell by the stripe on their sleeve what class they are in. Plebes don't have any. Youngsters have one slanted gold stripe on the left sleeve. A star and a horizontal gold stripe on both sleeves is worn by the first classmen. They also wear shoulder boards with the same stripes as are on their sleeves. They have anchors on their collars.

The Brigade of Midshipmen parading in full dress uniforms is a splendid sight to see at special times such as graduation. The brigade drills and drills to make their marching and formations perfect. Drills are held on Worden Field in the spring and fall on Wednesdays. You can watch about four thousand midshipmen march across the Yard and onto the field. Then they practice presenting arms and fixing bayonets. They march to the Academy band and the drum and bugle corps playing "Anchor's Aweigh" and the "Marine Hymn."

Drilling for parades is hard. It is even harder to get into the Naval Academy. Young men and women must be top students at their high

Parade drill on Worden Field.

The Brigade of Midshipmen in full dress. Both men and women
are called midshipmen.

school or preparatory school. They must be in excellent health. They must be honorable. Most important, they must be willing to go through the rough training of plebe year and later military training.

The Naval Academy is part of the U.S. Navy. Money to run the Academy is appropriated by Congress. It does not cost any money to go to the Academy. A student gets into the Academy by applying and then being appointed. The Academy's Admission Board okays an application. A congressman, a senator, or the president can appoint someone to the Academy. No one can enter unless they have both the appointment and the board's okay. Not everyone gets in; there is not room for all the young students who apply.

Most of the courses are in engineering, science, and mathematics. There are also courses in history and English. When a midshipman graduates, he or she receives a Bachelor of Science degree. Each one receives a commission as either a Navy ensign or a Marine second lieutenant. They pick the branch of service in which they want to serve. They also pick the type of work they want to do. They may want to be an aviator, a diver, or a doctor. The midshipman who ranks first in the class gets the work he picked. All the selections are based on order of class rank. Finally the Anchorman, who is the last in the class, is given whatever is left. They get extra schooling for the work they pick. They stay in the Navy or Marine Corps at least six years after graduation.

The midshipmen get training on ships, too. They always have done this. In the early days they climbed the rigging of the *Constitution*. Later on they trained in steam launches. Today they cruise in the summer. The plebes might spend four weeks sailing the forty-four-foot sloops. Midshipmen about to become first classmen cruise for four to eight weeks on big cruisers or destroyers. Some of them might even sail with a navy from another country. They all train at sea just as the old sailors knew they should.

When Franklin Buchanan was the Academy's first superintendent, he said honor and loyalty were most important for a midshipman.

Midshipmen getting seamanship training in the early 1900s, just as they always have done.

Honor means never cheating on an exam and always telling the truth. Loyalty means being true to the flag just as Commandant Rodgers said so long ago.

When someone enters the Academy, he or she takes this oath:

"I, . . . . . . . ., having been appointed a midshipman in the United States Navy, do solemnly swear (or affirm) that I will support and defend the Constitution of the United States against all enemies, foreign and domestic; that I will bear true faith and allegiance to the same; that I take this obligation freely, without any mental reservation or purpose of evasion, and that I will well and faithfully discharge the duties of the office on which I am about to enter, So Help Me God."

Ever since it started, the Naval Academy has graduated men and women who have brought honor to their country, in war and in peace. Whether they are in the Sports Hall of Fame, dared to try something new, or were heroes, they will not be forgotten. Here are some of them.

James E. Carter, 39th President of the United States
Albert A. Michelson, First American Nobel Prize winner for physics
Astronauts: Alan B. Shepard, Jr., Walter M. Schirra, Jr., William
    A. Anders, Charles F. Bolden, Jr., and Wendy Lawrence
Admiral William J. Crowe, former chairman, Joint Chiefs of Staff
Admiral Stansfield Turner, former director of the CIA
John S. McCain, III, Senator from Arizona
John H. Dalton, Secretary of the Navy
Roger Staubach, former quarterback, Dallas Cowboys
Joseph M. Bellino, Heisman Trophy winner
Montel Williams, TV talk-show host
David Robinson, basketball player, San Antonio Spurs

If you would like to learn more, visit your local library or the nearest bookstore. Ask to see books about the U.S. Navy and naval heroes.

# When Some Things Happened

1695   The little port of Annapolis is made the capital of Maryland.

1776   The Declaration of Independence is signed in Philadelphia, Pennsylvania.

1779   John Paul Jones is captain of the *Bonhomme Richard*. He fights the British ship *Serapis* and defeats it.

1821   The U.S. Navy starts a school for midshipmen in the ship *Guerriere*.

1845   George Bancroft is appointed Secretary of the Navy in March. On October 10 he opens the U.S. Naval School at Fort Severn.

1850   The school's name is changed to the U.S. Naval Academy.

1859   The Herndon Monument is erected in the Yard.

1861   The Civil War begins when Fort Sumter, South Carolina, is bombarded on April 12 and 13. The Academy is moved to Newport, Rhode Island, on April 26.

1865   The Civil War ends on April 9. The Academy is moved back to Annapolis. The classes reopen in October.

1866   The wooden figurehead Tecumseh is set up beside the Lyceum, the Academy's museum.

1883   The code of honor is broken when Charles E. Woodruff puts the answers to a math test on a door.

1890   The first Army-Navy football game is held.

1895  Architect Ernest Flagg is hired to design new buildings for the Yard.

1898  The battleship *Maine* blows up in Havana harbor.

1905  Ambassador Porter finds John Paul Jones's remains in Paris, France.

1907  "Anchor's Aweigh" is sung for the first time at an Army-Navy football game.

1909  The chapel's bronze doors designed by Evelyn B. Longman are unveiled.

1911  Lieutenant John Rodgers makes the first flight around the Yard.

1917  The United States enters World War I.

1939  Preble Hall is built as the new home for the Academy's museum.

1941  The Japanese attack Pearl Harbor, Hawaii, on December 7. The United States enters World War II.

1949  Wesley A. Brown is the first African American to graduate from the Academy.

1973  The new library at the Academy is dedicated to Chester A. Nimitz.

1976  The first women are admitted to the Academy.

1995  The Academy celebrates its 150th anniversary.

# Some Books Used to Write This Story

Anderson, Elizabeth B. *Annapolis: A Walk through History.* Centreville, Md.: Tidewater Publishers, 1984.

Benjamin, Park. *The United States Naval Academy.* New York: Putnam, 1900.

Chapelle, Howard I. *The History of the American Sailing Navy.* New York: Norton, 1935.

Edsall, Margaret Horton. *A Place Called the Yard.* Annapolis, Md.: Edsall, 1984.

Howarth, Stephen. *To Shining Sea: A History of the United States Navy, 1775–1991.* New York: Random House, 1991.

Mackenzie, Ross. *Brief Points: An Almanac for Parents and Friends of U.S. Naval Academy Midshipmen.* Annapolis, Md.: Naval Institute Press, 1993.

Stevens, William Oliver. *Annapolis—Anne Arundel's Town.* New York: Dodd, Mead, 1951.

Sturdy, Henry Francis. *Seeing Historic Annapolis and the Naval Academy.* N.p., 1961.

Sweetman, Jack. *The United States Naval Academy: An Illustrated History.* Annapolis, Md.: Naval Institute Press, 1979.

Warren, Mame, and Marion E. Warren. *Everybody Works but John Paul Jones.* Annapolis, Md.: Naval Institute Press, 1984.

# Index

# Picture Credits

The pictures in this book are used with the kind permission of the following:

U.S. Naval Academy Archives: pages 18 (Official U.S. Navy photo), 36, 43, 59, 61, 63 (Courtesy Joseph Martin), 73, 88, 90

U.S. Naval Academy Museum: page 8

U.S. Naval Academy Special Collections, Nimitz Library: pages 23, 25 (*top*), 55, 56, 66 (*top*); page 2 (*Heck's Iconographic Encyclopedia*); page 15 (from *Fag Ends*); page 25 (*bottom, Harper's Weekly*, May 11, 1861); page 35 (Sketch by C. G. Bush); page 49 (Robert E. Coontz Collection); page 65 (*Shakings*, Boston, 1867); page 66 (*bottom*, Pictorial Works, N.Y., E. H. Hart, 1890)

U.S. Naval Historical Foundation: page 6 (Sketch by William Partridge, 1817)

U.S. Naval Institute Photographic Library: pages 4, 5, 10, 16, 20 (*top*), 22, 33, 44, 45, 47, 51, 58, 68, 69, 70, 75, 76, 78, 81, 83, 84 (*bottom*), 87 (*top*), 92, 94, 95; page 20 (*bottom, Harper's New Monthly Magazine*); page 26 (*Harper's Weekly*, 1861); page 29 (Courtesy Dr. Walter B. LaBerge); page 31 (*Frank Leslie's Illustrated Newspaper*, 1861); page 38 (Painting by Gordon Grant); page 41 (Copyright *Photographic History of the Civil War*); page 54 (Sketch by Richard Rummell, 1908); page 87 (*bottom*, Illustration by Tom Jones); page 97 (Courtesy Rear Adm. Henry Williams)

# About the Author

I was born in Johnstown, Pennsylvania, on June 20, 1923. I wasn't there during the great, horrible flood, but many of my relatives were living in Johnstown then. When I grew up I went to Miami University in Oxford, Ohio. After I graduated I lived on farms in Ohio and Virginia. Then I went to live on a farm in Kent County, Maryland. I have lived in Tidewater, Maryland, ever since then. The farm I lived on had a big, old house, part of which was a log cabin. I was kept busy fixing up the house and tending the yard and flower gardens. I was kept busiest raising two lovely daughters. We liked living on the farm.

I began to write stories for children. My very first story was called "Bernard, the Buzz-less Bee," and was about a bee who decided to stop buzzing so he could fly anywhere without scaring people.

After a while I ran a children's clothing store, which gave me a good chance to meet a lot of children. But it didn't give me chance to make money, so I had to close it. Then I went to work at the Smithsonian Institution in Washington, D.C. I worked in the Natural History Building in the Department of Botany and then in the Department of Anthropology. I got to meet a lot of the special people–scientists, curators, artists, conservators–who take care of the enormous Smithsonian collections and make the exhibits possible. I wrote a children's book about the Smithsonian called *The Castle on the Mall,* and my friend Alice Tangerini illustrated it.

When it was time for me to retire I built a little house on a little creek near Chestertown, Maryland. I have a little garden. I can't have a big one because my land is full of trees that block out the sun. They help to keep the house cool. They also are home to all kinds of birds, and I have a fine time feeding and watching them. In the fall Canada geese come to my creek.

I began to write books about the young men who sailed the Chesapeake Bay and the Atlantic Ocean during colonial days. I spend a lot of time reading. I have always spent a lot of time reading. Now I volunteer as a tutor, teaching adults who never learned to read. I want them to enjoy books as much as I do.

I also travel as often as I can, often going by myself. I always plan the trip by reading about the history of the place where I'm going, its geography, and its tourist attractions. It's fun to plan a trip around a theme. Once I went to England to see many of the places that the first Queen Elizabeth knew, visited, or lived in.

Writing, reading, traveling, gardening, children, and mostly my family, these are what I like best.

THE NAVAL INSTITUTE PRESS

*The Story of the U.S. Naval Academy*

Designed and set by Pamela Lewis Schnitter
in Monotype Baskerville and Colonna on a Mac IIci

Text corrections made by Kelly Galla at Picas Rule,
Baltimore, Maryland

Text printed on 60-lb. Glatfelter A-50 by Maple-Vail Book
Manufacturing Group, York, Pennsylvania

Casesides printed on 80-lb. CS1 by
Phoenix Color Corporation,
Hagerstown, Maryland